Given to Change

GIVEN TO CHANGE

CHERYL STASINOWSKY

WORD SCRIBE

GIVEN TO CHANGE
Copyright © 2017 by Cheryl Stasinowsky

All rights reserved. No part of this book may be reproduced, stored in a retrieval system, or transmitted in any form or by any means-electronic, mechanical, photocopy, recording, or otherwise-without prior written permission of the copyright owner, except by a reviewer who wishes to quote brief passages in connection with a review for inclusion in a magazine, website, newspaper, podcast, or broadcast. Cheryl Stasinowsky does not capitalize the name of satan or any reference to the devil.

All Scripture quotations, unless otherwise indicated, are taken from the New King James Version of the Bible. Copyright © 1982 by Thomas Nelson, Inc.

Interior design and cover design provided by www.truenorthpublish.com.

Published by WordScribe.

ISBN: 978-0-9989233-0-7

For Worldwide Distribution. Published in the United States of America.

Dedication

I dedicate this book to my children. I have prayed for you every day of your life. I dedicate this book to my grandchildren and all generations after that. I might not ever meet you in person, but I want you to know that I am praying for you now. I am that praying grandma and great-grandma. I want you all to know that I have prayed into your future. I have not just lived focused on today, but I have purposed to change for you. I have worked on the past, to give you a better future. I leave you my faith and prayers and I want you to know that I love you and am thinking about you even now ...

My Family

I am "Given to Change" for them

Table of Contents

Acknowledgements
Endorsements
Introduction

Chapter 1: Expectations 23
Chapter 2: Positioning for a Change 29
Chapter 3: Not My Idea 33
Chapter 4: Change Your Thinking 39
Chapter 5: Change First 45
Chapter 6: Change the Past. 51
Chapter 7: Physical Change. 57
Chapter 8: Unexpected Change. 63
Chapter 9: Learn From Generations 69
Chapter 10: Heal the Generations. 73
Chapter 11: Let Them Live Life 77
Chapter 12: Heart Change 83
Chapter 13: Change Reveals 89
Chapter 14: Get the FEAR Out! 93
Chapter 15: Fast to Change. 99
Chapter 16: Testing Produces Change 105

Do You Need Jesus?
About the Author
More Titles by Cheryl Stasinowsky

Acknowledgements

Father, Son, and Holy Spirit

This book is evidence of Your work in me. Nothing in this book would even be possible or part of my life without You. You have personally taught me exceedingly and abundantly above all that I could ask or think. I love talking to You. I know You listen. I greatly appreciate Your constant availability to be in communication with me. Thank you for being 'Given' for me. I love You!

My Husband, Wally

Thank you for giving me the opportunity to write and minister to others. I am given to change for us and our relationship. Thank you for being patient with me through the process. I love you!

Amber and Daniel

I love you both! I have diligently been given to change for you and your future children. I hope I have modeled change and forgiveness to both of you. You will see generations that I will only get to change and pray for. What an honor to be a part of your lives.
I love you!

Jordan and Shelby

I love you both! I have learned that as I am willing to change and be open to new thoughts and ideas, our relationship grows. I will always be willing and open. I value our relationship and enjoy you both! Thank you for being patient with me through the process ...
I will continue to change me for you.
I love you!

Jean

Wow, another book. Every book I write is so much better after you go through and clean it up. I never knew so many commas were necessary. I love your little notes in the editing that always make me smile. May the Lord richly bless you for all the hours upon hours of reading and re-reading that you do.
You are a brilliant and humble editor
that I could not do without. Thank you!

Brian

Here we are, another book. You are wonderful to work with. I love how you listen to my visions for each book, and then, somehow, make it happen. You never complain or argue with me. You are a valuable asset to this team to make these books happen. Thank you!

Friends and Family

Thank you for all of your love, encouragement, and support over the years. It is a pleasure to write for you and share what I have learned. My books would go nowhere without you. Thank you for reading and sharing these books with your friends.
I am forever grateful to all of you!

Endorsements

Cheryl candidly, willingly shares personal insights and victories into the struggles of her life experiences in order that others might become victors in their own life struggles. Given to Change is but another great example of one whose life is completely committed to God for His working the changes needed to become the person He would have her to be, and Given to Change is the tool needed to help others be Given to Change, too. A great tool—a must read! Thank you, Cheryl.

Jean Hudak Kashella, Author, PA

I loved Cheryl's book because it spoke to my own inadequacies, i.e. fear of change, fear of losing someone, and how do I treat others in their fears and feelings. I found some of the same lessons learned as I leaned on Jesus to change me while in the state of fear. "Given to Change" allows us to share in Cheryl's walk into her change to a life of love for herself and others. Change never has to be fearful but will give new meaning to a life given to God the Father, God the Son, and God the Holy Spirit.

Rebecca Miller, CA

This book makes you stop and think, and evaluate your walk. It goes hand in hand with "Given to Forgive". I love "Given to Change".

Gale M. Kolb, Avid reader, CA

This book inspires a thoughtful reader onto a path, a highway of discovery, which is life changing. Thank you, Cheryl Stasinowsky. "Given to Change" has changed my life forever. I, also, highly recommend "Given to Love", "Given to Prayer" and "Given to Forgive".

Lynn Johnson, Sr. Chaplain, The Way Ministries, CA

Given to Change can be a very life changing book because it reveals the hidden issues of our heart if we allow it. It was truly a tipping point for me to see how little things can make a big difference if we are given to change. I highly recommend this as a bible study tool, also, as it truly opens up the eyes of our understanding regarding forgiveness and loving relationships.

Sandi Holman, prophetic intercessor, teacher
Sword of the Lord Ministries, TN

Given to Change is needed for every believer who is interested in changing the day to day lessons God wants us to uncover. There are hidden treasures all through the book and definitely will touch each life that takes the time to read it. Undeniably, the treasures I uncovered related to my life now, and for every reader that will probably hold true. I highly recommend that you dive in and uncover hidden treasures of your own.

Jessica Abersold, CA

Cheryl takes her readers on her personal journey of faith that has and will continue to change throughout the course of her lifetime. With each chapter she continually invites us not to be afraid of changes in our lives. Instead, we are to be open, embrace, and sometimes even initiate changes.

As she goes through different aspects of changes in her life, one theme has remained constant: forgiveness. Cheryl intertwines how vital practicing forgiveness is in order to claim victory in the changes of our lives. Without that, the victories are only temporary. In this book, Cheryl also walks us down the path that many of us are afraid of going: the path of vulnerability. But because of her faith in the forgiving work of Christ she is empowered to do it well, and should be an example to us all.

I implore you to invite the Holy Spirit to search your heart as you open up this book. Be vulnerable with Him. Be given to Him and He will bring about the change that your heart so desperately desires.

Joe Gadbaugh, OR

"Un-forgiveness gives fear a place to stay...and fear is the absence of God's love." These words moved mountains deep within my soul. Have you given yourself permission to hear His voice and to receive His love in a way that casts out every fear that entangles us?

Once again, Cheryl invites us into a sacred place that declares freedom where forgiveness and love abide. She writes a vulnerable story of wrestling through a transformative change that only Christ can give. As you read this book, I encourage you to embrace the challenge of being fully given to change!

Liz Gadbaugh, OR

Introduction

I have been asked what I mean by the word "Given". To me 'given' means committed to, submitted to, relentless pursuit; basically, I am 'all in' to the processes of God in my heart, soul, mind, and strength. I have not always been 'given', but over the years as I have asked Him to create in me a clean heart (Psalm 51:10), He has answered. It is not a one-time answer, but a daily, moment by moment, answer and process. I know that when I ask Him, He is 'given' to answer my prayer no matter how long it takes. As He untangles the mess of my past, I have grown to trust His process and love. To me, He has become the hiding place to which I run. I trust He is 'given' to me.

This book series is His work on cleansing my heart. The Lord gave me the titles prior to writing them, and little did I know or understand that I would be living the very books I would write. When I knew that the 'Given to Change' book was coming up next, I wondered what I would be walking through. Well, I was going to be walking through intense 'change'. I walked through physical change, mental change, emotional change, Spiritual change, heart change, generational change, and, most likely, change that I have not even been able to understand.

I was not normally a person who enjoyed change. I do not move my furniture around once it is placed. I do not try different roads to get to a location if I find one that works. I enjoy the security of knowing where things are, and I always put things back in the same place so I can find them. So, when it came to change, it made me uncomfortable and unsettled.

While writing this book, the Lord asked us to move and sell houses, and our son graduated from college and moved to another state. My entire safe, comfortable, country life got turned upside down and shaken up. Not only that, but He moved us back to the city we left 11 years prior. There is traffic, noise, stress, pressure, and I am a different person than I was when I left, so now I am trying to figure out how to do life with a different heart and mind. It has been quite a change and continues to be.

I am 'given' to His process of change even though it, at times, is painful, hard, challenging, frustrating, and yes, lonely. Every day, I submit to His plans and purposes, and at night, when I go to bed, I give the Father, the Son, and the Holy Spirit full permission to do whatever they need to do while I sleep. Yes, they work on some of my issues through my dreams. I am 'given' to Them because I like what They are doing on the inside of me. They know me better than I know myself. They know how I think, feel, process, struggle, and completely how I work inside.

This book is what I have learned about the processes of 'change'. They have been completely life-changing for me, and so I write to help others. These are not things I have learned in a book, but what I have walked through and have come out the other side. I have pressed into His Word to hear from Him. I have cried out to Him when I was so frustrated and did not understand and He answered. There is testimony and truth in this book that can change your heart towards God and others.

Please take time with this book and allow the Lord to minister to you through my stories and situations. When you begin to see His Hand in your life, you, too, will be 'Given' to Him. May you discover how 'given' He is to you as you read...

I am 'Given to Change'. Are you?

If you come across something in this book that you do not understand, write to me, I would love to try to clarify or explain further. My email address is at the back of this book...

CHAPTER 1
Expectations

We all have expectations, known and unknown, realized and unrealized, real or false, but we still have them. We expect people to act or be a certain way. We expect them to think and make decisions like we do. We expect people, at times, to read our mind. We expect people to be appreciative when we do something for them. We expect, and, many times, do not even realize we are expecting. All of this gets played out in our relationships with others. Guess what? They are doing this to us, too...

Where do our expectations come from? They come from our parents and upbringing. They can come from television shows and movies we watched growing up. They come from what we, personally, like and dislike. Sometimes they come from an unhealed hurt of our past, and we set up protection for the future. They, at times, get established within us and we do not realize it.

We discover our expectations when someone lets us down. We can think we do not have any expectations when we give something to or do something for someone, but if they do not respond or react like we felt they should, we can find ourselves frustrated or upset. Why? They did not receive what we did the way we expected them to receive. Did we communicate our expectations to them? Many times we do not. We might even tell them that we have no expectations, or even tell ourselves this, but the proof is in our reaction to their response or lack thereof.

This happens in marriage when two people say, "I do." Two people with expectations of marriage come together and discover the other person is not living up to their expectations. Do they call it this? Most likely, they do not even realize this is what is happening. They just know they are not happy and the other person is not meeting their needs or making them happy. If communication is poor, soon this marriage is in trouble and can fail, with each blaming the other for the failure. But, in many situations, it is unrealistic expectations not being met. The first mistake is, many times, the expectations are not even communicated, and the other person constantly has to learn the hard way. *If our expectations are not communicated to the other person, we really do not get to expect them.* I'm going to repeat that sentence. *If our expectations are not communicated to the other person, we really do not get to expect them.* It is not fair to the other person and brings frustration to both. Think about it...

EXPECTATIONS

This happens with our children, our in-laws, friendships, co-workers, leaders, and pretty much every relationship we have. Many times, the expectations we have of others are impossible to fulfill. I am not even sure we live up to our own expectations if we were totally honest with ourselves. Think about it...take time to think about your expectations of each person in the relationships you have that are struggling or have failed.

We all have needs and, many times, we are unaware we expect others to fulfill them. But what if the people around us are not the ones who can, nor are supposed to, fulfill our needs? What if the deep needs, desires, and expectations can only be fulfilled by God? What if we expect people to be who we want and need them to be, and people are not meant to be the ones to do this? If we are mad at God, or do not even know Him or have a relationship with Him, we will go through many relationships trying to get that need and expectation met. Yes, there might be a few people who will meet our expectations, but not many. Think about your relationships in your past...what went wrong? What went right? Did you expect something that should not have been expected of them? Were your expectations realistic?

I have, personally, been re-evaluating my expectations of others. I have let go of what an ideal relationship should be, because the truth is, I do not live up to my own expectations that I have of others. I have forgiven them and asked the Lord to forgive me, and I have forgiven myself. I am learning to have realistic expectations of people and not try to make them be who I want them to be, and let them be who they are to be...guess what, we are also on the receiving end of this...Think about it, make a change, get real, be aware of what you are expecting, forgive, and make a new plan...your relationships will thank you!

CHAPTER 2
Positioning for Change

There are mornings when I wake up overwhelmed with life, or anxious, or just flat where I cannot seem to figure out where God is, and I definitely cannot hear Him. There are times when the cares of life press in and start to win. There are times when I do not have a great positive attitude. I am not fond of mornings like this, and I certainly do not want to carry how poorly I am feeling and thinking into the rest of my day, so I position myself to change.

Every morning, I get my cup of coffee, turn on the worship music, whether it is in my ears or through a speaker, I prop up my pillows and I open my Bible and try to find a place that begins to change my thinking, if even just slightly. Some days this is very easy, and I wake up happy and filled with faith, but I do the same thing. But on the days like I described above, it takes effort. I go to where I am in my normal reading, and if I cannot get my mind to connect with it, I go searching elsewhere in my Bible. I have favorite chapters and so I try those. I have highlighted verses and I turn page after page until something shifts my thoughts, attitude, feelings, and I can discover God is still around that day. I talk to Him, at times, even crying out to Him to help me.

I try to find things to be thankful for when I am focusing on all the wrong. I try to submit myself and everything about my life to God and I resist the poor thinking, inaccurate understandings, the lies, the fears, the sickness, the lack of motivation, and it eventually flees. What am I doing? I am positioning myself to change.

In Proverbs 23:7 the first line states, "For as he thinks in his heart, so is he." I purpose to get my thinking about my life, myself, my day, and my God in a positive direction. Sometimes this takes a long time, and other times it is not very long. Sometimes I have to go on a walk listening to worship music and purpose to focus on the words being sung. I have favorite worship songs and so I listen to those.

Sometimes un-forgiveness is the problem, and so I go to work on that. I forgive anyone the Holy Spirit brings to mind. I am pretty relentless to get as close to God as I can get each day. I want His word to direct my thoughts, my actions, my words, the way I hear, the way I see, and everything about me.

Sometimes I have to turn off my phone so it does not distract me. There are times when this feels like an all-out war but I will not give into it. I will not get up from this pressing in without a change in my heart and mind. I do not like who I am if I give into how I felt when I woke up. I know some have to go to work. Get up early, and listen to worship music the whole time you are getting ready; listen to His word while you drive. You are going to change your day one way or another, for the good or for the bad, and the outcome of your day begins with what you do about how it starts, and also, how you are thinking.

I, particularly, love Psalm 119. I read it slowly and pay attention to the words. I come into agreement with them and make it my prayer. In that Psalm, you will discover the phrase, "Your word" 38 times...His word is very powerful and it can change the worst of our attitudes. When I read His word every day, I position myself to change. It reads my heart. It brings truth to the lies I believe. It brings understanding to situations I am facing. He speaks directly to my heart and mind things I did not even know I needed. When I read His word, I'm learning about whom He is and who He is to me and in me. I am learning about who He created me to be and what I can do. For me, when I read His word, it is like plugging into the wall socket and recharging my battery.

I cannot allow a day to go by that I do not do this. I love who I am after my time with Him. He changes my perspective and gives me wisdom. I need fresh revelation every day regardless of how I feel or think. I cannot allow my poor attitude to rule in my thinking. A vital part of my everyday life is positioning myself to change and maybe even admitting that it is necessary ...

CHAPTER 3
Not My Idea

One of the biggest changes that came in my life was on one evening in February when I was filled with the Holy Spirit. I had no idea how big a change that would be when I said yes. It took me 2-1/2 years to finally be fully given to change, or so I thought. My change was rapid. I went from working in our construction business 60 to 70 hours a week, to five overnight. I went from watching 3 to 4 hours of television every night to zero. I went from eating food to find comfort to eating food of which I did not know (John 4:32). His Word went from being a history book to a living book. Everything changed...

Over the last 6 years, I have been struggling to believe that I was an author. It does not matter how many books I have published, or how many people tell me that I am an author, I still did not see myself as one. It has been a deep struggle. Here is my process...

With each book that I published, the struggle inside of me remained. I began to realize that when I was a general contractor, I believed I was one because of the amount of money we made, and also, the amount of money that people were willing to pay us to do their job. We made a lot of money. People also seemed to respect us because of our success. I am not sure if this is actual or perceived. I am not sure if I was different so people were different. But writing books does not bring the same result for me. Inside, I keep thinking that I am not an author until I sell millions of books. I do not talk about this very much because I find that people do not understand why I do not see myself as an author with 8 published books.

I have tried all the mental battles of being grateful for one sale. I have purposed not to focus on the numbers but on those to whom the books are ministering. I have tried to convince myself it is not about the sales or money…it is not about the success or being known…it is not about being recognized or being important, but my insides were still struggling with it. I thought it was because I did not have a big-name publisher like others, or because I did not get a huge advance of money to write a book, like in the movies or like bestselling authors. If I were brutally honest, I was embarrassed that I was an author according to my sales. When I started self-publishing, although I enjoyed the ability to make the book how I wanted, I felt even less than an author. I have not been able to figure out how to see myself any different.

I repented and asked the Lord to forgive me; I forgave myself…but still the struggle. I have spent hours with the Lord over this struggle. I thought maybe it was because I never saw myself as an author or I did not have a college education to be a writer. I have been discontent. I love writing with the Lord. It is very fulfilling, but something inside of me was not right. I struggled with viewing myself as a writer/author.

My son even asked me one time why I wrote books. I did not really have an answer for him. If I were even more brutally honest, I thought that someday someone important is going to get ahold of one of my books and tell everyone about it, and then, I will be an author. It is embarrassing to write about this, but I experienced a significant life change, and I could not figure out how to embrace it and allow it to be who I am and appreciate it.

One Sunday morning during worship at church, the Lord spoke to me, "You are an author. I have made you an author. I call you an author. Whether or not you are an author is not dependent upon how many books you sell. Your books are not selling in large quantities because this is not settled inside of you. Who you are and what you do cannot be dependent upon the success the world offers."

I asked Him how I get this settled inside of me; You know that I have been struggling with this for a very long time. I would love to write that it was settled then and there inside of me, but it was not.

Early the next morning, I approached the Lord with this area again. I want this settled once and for all. I thought maybe I needed to write it on a 3 x 5 card and carry it with me to remind myself that I am an author and teacher of His word. I realized this was just trying to convince myself, not believing it. As I sat there with Him, I finally saw that I was having trouble believing this because it was not my idea. This was not something I ever aspired to be. I was evaluating the success of the books to see if I wanted to embrace the title of author. I saw that, as I was doing this, I was actually despising the very gift God had given me. Do not get this wrong; I know I am a child of God. I know who I am in Him, but I was having a challenge with who He was calling me to be.

As I looked back over the last couple days, I was asking the Lord to teach me how to love Him more. That is when He began to show me how I felt about how He made me and the gifts He had given me. I was not finding value in them. I did not love who He made me to be, and it was hindering an area of my love for Him. I began repenting for my pride in thinking I knew better than He. I repented for thinking my life needed to be my idea. I repented and asked the Lord to forgive me for waiting to own that title as to whether it is a success or not. I, then, saw that I had been deciding if I wanted to own who I was based on my perceived value of success, which would be book sales and speaking engagements. I realized I was never going to achieve this because the enemy had it, and he was always moving the measuring rod I was using. I deeply sought forgiveness and I forgave myself for not embracing the change He had made in my 14 years prior. Guess what? I am an author and teacher of the Word of God.

I now see that we embrace change when it is our idea, and can resist change when we do not feel that we chose it, even if it is best for us. Do you have areas where He has changed you and you are not fully embracing the change? Spend some time with the Lord asking Him...I was very unsettled inside of me. No one understood it, but God did. I pray you get free to walk in the fullness of who He created you to be...

CHAPTER 4
Change Your Thinking

Most of us have had significant people in our lives, whether it is our parents, grandparents, leaders, maybe even employers. They are supposed to be there, we look up to them, learn from them, and either grow up wanting to be like them or not be like them. Hopefully, there is a healthy balance to counteract those who have been a negative influence in our lives.

I want to address the negative influences in our past. Maybe we had a parent who was abusive, angry, cursed at us, or was controlling and did not treat us well. Or maybe we had a leader who manipulated and controlled us. Whoever it was, if you had one, you know exactly who and what I am talking about. They, most likely, popped into your head just reading this. You cannot get their negative voice out of your head. You walk into a store and you hear their voice telling you what you should or should not get. You find them in your thoughts all the time. No matter how hard you try to get rid of the thoughts, they just keep surfacing within your daily life. Yes, those people.

If we grew up with people like this, or cross paths for any amount of time with people like this and we do not forgive them for what they did, then the offenses remain with us. That is why they continue to speak to us in negative ways even after they have passed away or we no longer associate with them. What they did to us or said to us is still inside of our heart and mind, repeating the offense over and over. This influences our thinking, and unfortunately, the very person we made vows to never be like, we are more similar to them than we realize. Why? Because we allowed what they did to us to remain inside of us by not forgiving. We might not totally realize it has happened, but every once in a while we will recognize the voice or words coming out of us as that person's. No matter how hard we try, we cannot shake it or change.

If we really have an issue with the person, then we begin having issues with ourselves because we are like them, but we take it out on others. The only way to begin changing this is to forgive them. You do not have to go to the other person. You sit with God and begin forgiving them for as many things as come to your mind. You might discover resistance because this has now become the way that you think. Keep forgiving and ask the Lord to forgive them and you, and finally forgive yourself. This will begin shutting down the voice and videos in your head. For me, with some of the people of my past, I have had to work on this for years. Whenever I would hear their voice or preference in my head, I would forgive. I wanted them out of my head. I no longer wanted to be controlled or influenced.

If we do not do this, permanent change is nearly impossible. In John 20:23, Jesus addresses it, "If you forgive the sins of any, they are forgiven them, if you retain the sins of any, they are retained." The word retain communicates that they stay inside of us until we forgive. Jesus is not saying that we now get to play God and choose who gets to be forgiven from His perspective, but He is telling us that if we do not forgive, what they did remains inside of us. We come into agreement with the sin and it influences us. Un-forgiveness is sin. There is no list of what is to be forgiven and not forgiven. Everything qualifies. If we retain it, we then allow it to, potentially, be given to our children and grandchildren. The very thing that we despise; in some cases, we do, and we hand down. Today would be a great day to change this…if you need more help on understanding forgiveness, I encourage you to get my book Given to Forgive, this revelation in this chapter was learned after the writing of that book.

Maybe you are older like I am, and you are just now learning this. It is not too late to change the future generations. Begin forgiving so that the Lord can begin to change how you think, and to change your perspective so the un-forgiveness stops and forgiveness begins. Be brave, go to your children and grandchildren and repent. Tell them what you have learned and what you did...change generation's one person at a time... Stop retaining and begin repairing...

Oh, I pray that generations will improve instead of be destroyed from the inside out. Maybe you are like me and hear your children repeat something you have said, and it was not positive. Recognize your part in it before telling them to stop what they are doing and even disciplining them for it. Take responsibility for yourself and repent with the Lord. Forgive yourself and your child. Then, take this as an opportunity to go to your child and explain what happened and what you did, and then, teach them about forgiving, asking them to forgive you for teaching them that. The Lord will reveal even our poor attitudes through our children. Taking responsibility changes generations!

CHAPTER 5
Change First

A while back, I was sitting with the Lord complaining about my husband, Wally. Yes, I fight being critical and everything else. So, as I was complaining, the Lord told me that everything I am complaining about, I created. Over the years, my words and actions have contributed to who he is today. So, if I wanted him to change, I had to change first. Yikes, that is not what I wanted to hear. I wanted God to agree with me. He showed me I had dug in my heels and was determined to change when he changed, but the fact was...I needed to change first.

I began working on me. I started forgiving him every day. Not to his face, but in my time with the Lord, I would purpose to forgive him and ask the Lord to forgive him, and then ask the Lord to forgive me, and I forgave myself. I also began reading and studying 1 Corinthians 13, and as I saw how I was the clanging cymbal, I began to pray and make this chapter my prayer guide and heart's cry to the Lord. I took that determined individual inside of me and made her purpose to change the way He showed me to change. I gave Him full permission to work on me. I got my eyes and energy off of trying to change Wally and put it into changing me. I quit blaming and took responsibility for my part.

I learned that being still and knowing that He is God meant that I needed to be still with my mouth. I was amazed as I started to do this, as then I would hear my thoughts of what I would have said, and it was not good. Those little digs and comments that break down the other person are not a joke to them. Yes, we can convince ourselves that we are just kidding, but are we? As I was truthful with me about me, I began to change.

One of the toughest things the Lord asked me to do was when He wanted me to take the next thirty days, and each day I was to write 10 positive things about my husband. Yes, different things each day. Yes, that is 300 positive things about my husband. I am sad to say that it seemed impossible. I told my husband about it and he said that it would be easy for him to do that for me. I felt even worse. So, the first day was pretty easy to find 10 positive things about him. I wrote them down. The Lord asked me to send them to my husband to build him up. I was surprised at the resistance I felt to do this. I had more forgiving to do. Un-forgiveness keeps us from wanting to build up others that we have it towards (might be a warning sign to some of a heart condition). The next day was more difficult. I had to really pay attention to what he did during the day to come up with the 10 new things. Can you see what the Lord was doing? He was changing my focus. Because of un-forgiveness I had become critical and only looked at everything he did wrong. By purposing to come up with the 10 new things each day, I had to look for them. It worked. By the end of the 30 days, I was seeing what an amazing man he was, and he got built up in the process.

It was, and continues to be, a valuable season in my life and our marriage. As I forgave all the little things that I had held against him, I began to see him. As my heart was healing, our marriage was healing. Un-forgiveness kept me blaming my husband for everything. I controlled, put down, and did not love him as the Lord intended.

Another touchy area for me was Ephesians 5:22, "Wives, submit to your own husbands, as to the Lord." So many times when a male pastor would teach on this section of the Bible, all the wives in the room would cringe, and the men, inside, were thinking, preach it.

I know inside of me, I was not going to submit to a man that did and said the things he had done (un-forgiveness). I would submit to him when he lined up with the rest of the verses about him. Submission, in my mind, was to just give in and do whatever he said. Submission, in my mind, was being a doormat and saying nothing. It was a very negative word to me. I would avoid this verse and skip to all the verses about him, and evaluate him through these verses, and justify why I did not have to submit. Yes, I had an issue with submitting, I was in process of changing first, and this verse hit me right between the eyes.

Here is what the Lord showed me about Ephesians 5:22-33...both the husband and the wife are accountable to God as to their behavior towards one another. There is no "if he" or "if she", then "I will" in these verses. It is not conditional upon the behavior of the other person. I did not really like this. I did not like this word submit at all. Then the Lord showed me what He means by submit... Wives submit to loving, helping, encouraging, praying, strengthening, and building up your husbands. Yikes, epic fail. When I looked at how the Lord intended this verse, it was no longer negative. I also realized that my actions influence his actions. I saw my part in all of this. I saw how, over the years, I had discouraged more than encouraged, torn down instead of building up...He had become who I created him to be, one negative comment, action, and look at a time.

I repented to the Lord and to my husband (quite humbling). I also had to forgive myself. You see, when I got to verse 28, "So husbands ought to love their own wives as their own bodies; he who loves his wife loves himself." Yikes, I had torn him down so much over the years; he did not stand a chance to love himself, which, in turn, made it very difficult to love me. I went to work on this quickly and prayerfully...

Relationships change us for the good or the bad, it is our choice. The other person makes mistakes and so do we... forgiveness is the key to change in the positive direction.

Un-forgiveness over the years will make us selfish and that is very destructive in a relationship, married or not... it also affects our relationship with Jesus...

So, if you have someone in your life that you might be upset with or blaming, take a look at yourself...forgive the other person, forgive yourself, and begin changing yourself first as you might be the problem and not even know it. It takes courage. It takes determination. It takes time, but it is worth it...change first...

CHAPTER 6
Change the Past

I stood there in shock as my husband, of four days, told me that he did not like roller coasters and did not have to ride them anymore. What? We dated for 4-1/2 years and we went on many roller coasters (I love them), and you went on them every time with me. How can you take me to an amusement park, on our honeymoon, stand in line for a roller coaster ride and tell me that, and then get out of line and watch me go on the ride? This moment, over 35 years ago, turned my world upside down.

I came from a home where my trust had been broken repeatedly. Promises had been broken, lies had been told, and so I had a trust issue (lots of un-forgiveness). So, when my new husband told me this truth, I felt betrayed, and he went into the untrustworthy box of my life. This was not a good way to begin a marriage. We were very young and did not know much about forgiveness. Little did I know that for much of our marriage, that moment was at the root of all my cross examinations of my husband. I did not trust him. I did not believe him, and my actions, comments, questions, subtle looks, and my heart all were influenced by that moment. It has affected my children as well, because they saw much of what I did and, of course, they learned it.

What could I have done differently? I should have forgiven him on the spot. I should have asked the Lord to forgive him. I should have asked the Lord to forgive me, and I should have forgiven myself. This would have closed the door to my years of trust issues with him. This would have closed the door to always wondering if there were other things about which he was lying.

Because I did not forgive in that moment, I opened a door to being critical, judgmental, controlling (because I was afraid and did not trust), and many other negative things. This created many issues in our marriage that could have been completely avoided by forgiving in that moment, and the next moment, and every moment after that. I will be completely honest, I am just realizing this after 35 years of marriage, and 10 years of working on and learning about forgiving (read Given to Forgive).

I have to keep forgiving myself because I could have prevented so much heart ache...Un-forgiveness got the best of our past because it kept me blaming him for all of the issues. But as I have been working on clearing out my un-forgiveness, I can see my part in all of it. Yes, he had a part in it as well, but I am accountable for mine and he is accountable for his. I'm just sad about it. I let the enemy win by choosing not to forgive in the moment.

When I forgave for that moment in that line, the blame lifted, the thoughts of him being untrustworthy began to go away, and my perspective of life began to change completely. How can un-forgiveness have such strength that it can change a future? It can because we come into agreement with the enemy who is out to steal, kill, and destroy (John 10:10) everything about our life. The enemy has learned that un-forgiveness is his most effective weapon. It is sad that the Bible is filled with teaching us to forgive, and yet, we seem to miss the value in forgiving.

I am writing this chapter to help others who might be at the beginning of marriage, or even in the middle of a challenging one. Maybe you are like me, and have spent many years blaming and being critical, and you cannot figure out how to stop it, or you believe lies that it is entirely their fault. I want to help you change your past so you think differently in your present, and then you are given to change in your future. What we do today will be our past tomorrow...so change your past today...do you have a moment that has popped into your mind as you were reading this? Forgive and watch what happens...

When I forgave, my perspective and understanding of the past changed. I discovered this had happened with many people over the years and relationships got damaged on both sides from un-forgiveness. I am spending, and plan to spend, the rest of my life forgiving the past, and forgiving quickly in the present. Maybe you are on the receiving end of it, like my husband was. The way I treated him affected him, but he began forgiving me, too.

We each have a past we bring into a relationship; forgiveness is the way through all of it. Teach your children to be good forgivers so they have a different future. You see, changing my past is changing my future and that of my future generations. Take some time changing your past, as I have changed mine ...

CHAPTER 7
Physical Change

We might not always have a choice in how our physical bodies are changing, but we do have a choice in our response to it. We all encounter change every day with our bodies as they grow older. If we work in a physical capacity and we are not used to it, we will become sore. When we make a decision to change our body and join a gym, we first encounter pain. Our environment around us gives us many opportunities to change for the good and for the bad. Take a look at your life in this chapter, what are you resisting? What are you giving in to? Are you aware that you are changing?

At the moment, I get to encounter hot-flashes many times a day. If you have had them before or are encountering them now, then you know what I am talking about when I tell you that they are very uncomfortable and uncontrollable. You can be fine one minute and the next minute you are so hot that you want to pull your skin off.

They do not last very long for me, but they seem like a long time. I started thinking of them as the Refiner's Fire being turned up in a moment and all of my stuff coming to the surface. In this moment, self-control has to be my choice or I will be extremely irritable, impatient, and frustrated. I have to make myself choose to be still and know that He is God until they pass. Sometimes they are so intense that my glasses steam up. I have even felt claustrophobic in my own skin. I have to resist reacting and being irritable or rude to others when they happen.

I remember when I was pregnant, sorry men, and I would hear people tell me that I now get to eat anything I want. I am going to gain weight anyway, so at least enjoy it. That never made sense to me because I was, then, going to be stuck with that decision after I had the baby. I would, then, have to exercise and monitor my eating even more. After nine months, poor eating habits would be formed, and I would have to fight them and change them. Besides the fact that it was not healthy for me or the baby.

We hear of men going through a 'mid-life crisis'...are they real? I'm not sure I get to judge that, but what they do with it is important. Does this become their excuse to do whatever they want and blame this label?

As I said at the beginning, there are many physical changes that we encounter, and we do not always have a choice in some of them, but we all have a choice in how we react to them. If I am tired or stressed, I do not want that to be an excuse for me to be rude or disrespectful

PHYSICAL CHANGE

to another person. Ultimately, we are all responsible for ourselves and our choices and behavior. We need to be aware of the influence.

Maybe we have a challenging co-worker, or a non-paying tenant, or it is our time of the month...maybe we injured ourself or became sick...maybe a stressful job situation or we did not have enough sleep...sometimes we encounter change in our physical bodies that are out of our control, especially as we grow older, but we need to allow our bodies to change and not allow the change to influence us to have a negative reaction to it and to others around us in the moment.

Through my hot-flashes, I chose to be thankful for who God made me to be and how my body is changing. If I am around others, I hold onto self-control. I try to eat healthier and exercise. This might sound odd, but I continually work on my heart with forgiving so that when the fire gets turned up inside of me, what comes out is not un-forgiveness. If my body is changing, then I am going to be given to the change and allow it to refine me into a better person.

I work on forgiving all the time, because I know that it has the potential to influence me to look for any excuse to be rude, disrespectful, frustrated, ungrateful, and many other things that are the result of un-forgiveness and seem to want to come out with some type of physical change. I try very hard not to give in to reacting, but rather, to respond with prayer and self-control. When I am given to change, a positive result can be the conclusion. Think about what you are going through. Do you allow yourself to react or respond...is it changing you for the better or to be bitter? I want to be given to change to become better...I do not want to allow myself to use change to give me an excuse for a choice I would not normally make. Partnering with God and forgiveness brings the best result in physical change...

CHAPTER 8
Unexpected Change

I sit here writing on the eve of Easter, the day that is between the death and resurrection of Jesus Christ (John 18-20, Luke 22-24, Mark 14-16, Matthew 26-28). This is such an interesting view as I sit with the Disciples in the middle of an unexpected change between the death and resurrection. It was not unexpected to Jesus, and He even tried to tell His Disciples it was coming, but they did not understand.

Their world got turned upside down at the death of Jesus. The man they had given everything up for and had been with for the last three years of their lives was dead.

Did their dreams die? Did their hope die? We know what happened, but they did not. Can you join me, right here in the middle of a horrible, devastating moment in time where the Disciples have no idea what to do?

Death, definitely stings deeply for all of us. We all encounter this unexpected change in our lives whether it is the death of a parent, or family member, a spouse, a close friend, a child, a relationship, a pet, a dream or business, a home...whatever it is, the feelings and emotions are similar. It just plain hurts so deeply that life stops, and, somehow, you have to figure out how to start again. Yes, there are varying degrees of emotion, dependent upon the level of the relationship that death removed from us. Life completely changes, and no matter how prepared we feel we are, until we are in the middle of it, we do not know how lonely and empty it can be.

So much is seemingly dumped upon us in an instant. I know there are many books out there on grief, but this is one chapter that has some helpful tools and understanding that have worked for me. I, personally, have experienced the sudden death of my brother-in-law, my dad, all of my grandparents, pets, dreams, a business, my life as I knew it, divorce of my parents, my children growing up and going off on their own, and I have walked through death with others.

It is painful. Each of these situations and more finds everyone in the middle of the death and resurrection, the difference is the amount of time it takes to walk in the new life that was not chosen by us, with the pain of the loss that can never be gotten back (in the case of physical death).

How do we respond? How do we not avoid caring deeply and risk the pain or potential of it again? What about the regrets, the reconciliation that never came, the apologies never spoken? What about that void inside? What about the confusion, fear, and hopelessness that knocks on the door in the middle of the night? What about the missing of the sound of their voice or the touch of their hand? Come on, connect in, this is where the Disciples are...

I would suggest letting it happen...the tears, the grief, the deep sorrow...let it out...the more we try to avoid it, or shove it down and ignore it, the more damage we are causing inside of our heart and mind and the longer the process can become. Is this easy? Absolutely not, but it is necessary. Tears can come in a moment's notice; it is okay to let them flow. If you are with someone who is walking this, let them cry. It is a little uncomfortable, but the more comfortable we can be with them crying, the more healing they will get. If you do not have any words to say, then say nothing, just be with them and cry with them if that is your response. Tears are so cleansing and they help us release the pain. This is for both men and women. If you need to talk about the death, then talk about it; find someone who is a good listener. The more you can let it out, the less you are holding inside.

There is another area that I have found very necessary and that is forgiving. When a death happens, we want to blame someone for it, maybe God, or another person or even ourselves. Recognize whom you are blaming, and as quickly as possible, begin forgiving. Anger will come knocking on your door and forgiving is the sign you place on that door. As we forgive, God brings healing. This process can take days, months or years, it depends on the person and circumstances, but the process applies to all. Forgive, forgive, forgive..., I am not saying this is easy, and you definitely will not feel like doing this; it is a choice. Are you still with me?

Maybe things between you and the other person never got resolved, regret and guilt will also be joining anger at that door, forgive. Maybe you said things that you wish you had not...forgive yourself. Maybe you did not tell them you loved them or got to say good-bye...forgive yourself. Maybe you are mad at God...forgive Him and then forgive yourself. The why's, what's, how's, and unanswered questions...talk it out with God.

If we do not forgive and get God in our process of this unexpected change, then it takes much longer. He has the answers. He knows what to do. He knows exactly what you need and when you need it. He knows the pain. He understands and will never leave you alone for a moment. But when we experience this death, the enemy does everything he can to get us away from God's help. What do you think would have happened to Judas if he had just waited a couple more days? Look at Peter, he denied knowing Jesus three times and heard the rooster crow and ran off in shame. Judas did not forgive himself and did not experience the resurrection. Do not walk away from Him in the middle of the death and resurrection of your very life.

UNEXPECTED CHANGE

Another unexpected change is the change that occurs when we fully give our lives to Jesus. We might have ourselves convinced that we have it all together and everything is fine, and not even realize how selfish we are. Fourteen years ago, I encountered the Holy Spirit after being a Christian for twenty years prior. As the Holy Spirit began to reveal areas within me not healed from my past, I was shocked. I experienced unexpected change in my heart, my thoughts, my actions, the way I heard others, and the way that I spoke and treated others, as I forgave myself and others in my past (read my book Given to Forgive, if you haven't already)...it was an unexpected change that was very positive as I died to self and started to walk in who He created me to be and not what the hurts of life had created me to be. This is when I became GIVEN to forgive first, then GIVEN to Love next, which enabled me to be fully GIVEN to Prayer, which is now helping me to be more fully GIVEN to Change and embrace it no matter how it comes...

Death is an unexpected change; how we embrace it affects our way through it. We do get through it, and I promise you, Jesus is right there with you whether you acknowledge Him or not. Forgiveness is the best gift we can give ourselves when we encounter an unexpected change ...

CHAPTER 9
Learn From Generations

A while back, I was having challenges with my teenage son. He was not able to forgive his father and me for a decision we made when he was eleven. According to him, that decision ruined his life. No matter how many times we apologized to him, he just could not let it go. Many times he would remind us of how we made a poor decision. Of course, we would respond with rationalization and justification as to why. We could not ask an eleven year old if we should shut down our business and go to ministry school, it was not his decision to make, so we felt justified in our decision and he felt unimportant and unheard.

This went on for several years. One day, I realized I, too, was feeling this way about my mom. There were decisions she made in my childhood that I felt were detrimental to my upbringing. I paid attention to what I was thinking and wanting from her. I did not want to hear, what seemed to me, as excuses as to why things happened; I just wanted her to take responsibility for what it did to me. I realized that is what my son needed to get from us. He did not need to hear any reasoning, but just that we were sorry for ruining his life. I wrote him an email, he lived in Florida, and kept it short, and apologized for the decision we made and how it had affected him. I never heard back from him in regards to that email, but he has not brought it up since, and he seems to be much more accepting of us. I was learning from generations...

I, then, began looking at my relationship with my mom. Because of circumstances we never really bonded as mother and daughter. I had a wonderful relationship with my daughter; and so, I started paying attention to how she was treating me and honoring me as her mother. I began trying to do those types of things for my mom. My daughter would send me a text message telling me she loved me, and I would then send one to my mom. The more I became aware of this, the more I was trying it, and it was changing our relationship. I was learning from generations...

My husband was finding it hard to have conversations with our son. Our son was calling me all the time, but not him. I encouraged him to look at his relationship with his dad. What is it that challenges him when he is on the phone with his dad? What did he wish his dad would say to him? He started giving to our son what he wished his dad would give to him. He would listen better and give less advice. He would, on purpose, stay on the phone and not find a way or get distracted to get off the conversation. It started to work; our son was calling him more often and the conversations were good. He was learning from generations...

This has now become a way of learning for both my husband and I as we learn in both directions how to give to our children what we desire for our parents to give to us, and we give to our parents what we desire for our children to give to us. This has changed all of our relationships. We have learned how to honor better. We have learned how to pay attention to what works and what does not work for us. We give far less advice and we listen far more. We allow our children to live their lives, and we do not get involved in their decisions unless we are asked. I would encourage you to take some time and look both ways in the generations you are between and see if there is something valuable to learn...learn and change...

CHAPTER 10
Heal the Generations

Not only can we learn from generations, as in the previous chapter, but we can bring healing to generations after us. In Exodus chapter 20:5, we are informed of the consequences of sin. If we do not deal with our own sin, the consequences do not just remain with us, but they get passed down to the third and fourth generations. We do not have to believe this to be true.

Let me give you an example...my two children did not get along very well. I was constantly trying to get them to get along, to stop fighting and forgive, and everything else I could think of, but still, the constant fighting and bickering. I finally went to the Lord and asked Him why they continually struggle to get along. He showed me how my brothers and I did not get along, how my dad and his sister did not get along, how my mom and her brother had challenges with getting along. He recalled stories I had heard about my grandmother and grandfather not getting along with their siblings. It did not stop there. He, then, showed me the challenges my husband had with his siblings, his parents with their siblings, and his grandparents with their siblings.

This had been going on for many years and kept getting passed down to the next generation. I saw it, and now to address it and get it to stop! I repented for not getting along with my brothers and asked the Lord to forgive me. I forgave my brothers and asked the Lord to forgive them. I forgave myself. I, then, did this with my parents, forgiving them for the challenges they had with their siblings, and asked the Lord to forgive them and me, and I forgave myself. I did the same for my grandparents.

I, then, asked the Lord to break the generational curse that kept getting passed down from generation to generation, and I asked Him to bless the generations with love, agreement, laughter, hope, blessing, and peace. My husband did the same on his side of the family. (Even though some of these generations have passed away, the generational consequences still continue until repentance and forgiveness takes place.)

Then, I waited to see how it was going to change. I had no conversation with my children about this. I am not kidding you, they get along great now. To me, it is a miracle, to them, it is natural. The generations, in regards to siblings, have been healed and the curse stopped. My heart and attitude toward my brothers, also, was healed.

HEAL THE GENERATIONS

Generations are changed by forgiveness...do you notice anything repeating generation after generation? Maybe you need to spend a little time and work on it like I did. It is as if the thread that was holding everyone to the same choice of contention was cut, and we laugh, and enjoy each other. In the future, my grandchildren will have the advantage of getting along together...

CHAPTER 11
Let Them Live Life

I remember the moment I handed the responsibility of choices to my teenage daughter. She came to me asking if she could go somewhere, and my response was, "What do you think?" She looked at me puzzled. I asked her if she had thought through the choice, and so, the discussion began of her learning how to make responsible choices in life on her own, but under the safety of our care and guidance. I will tell you that it was one of the most challenging times of my life, and yet, the most freeing at the same time. She had to choose if it was a good decision to go or not to go and learn how to evaluate her choices. It was a significant shift for both of us.

When our children are very young, we, as parents, teach, help, protect, love, discipline, and pretty much control where they go and what they do. If we do this the entire time they are in our home, we hinder their growth as adults. They start out life completely dependent upon us for their every need, but our role as the parent is to equip them for success in life as an adult. That means that as we shift the responsibility to them, we need to allow them to learn through mistakes and successes. Yes, we have lots of life experience, but it is our experience and not theirs. They learn much quicker, as it becomes their experience with their choice. To do this, parents, we have to change with them as they change …

As they get older, we get out of their way. We need to allow them to make mistakes. We need to allow them to learn. We no longer tell them what to do, but allow them to discover that on their own, and we become a resource if they ask us. We need to avoid controlling and criticizing their choices, to supporting and being there for them as they learn. It is similar to when they were learning how to walk. Remember those first steps…as they tried, we encouraged them to try again. As they get older, we change for them and become their biggest fan. We believe in them when no one else does, including themselves.

I have had moments with both of my grown children where life seemed over as they walked through disappointments or failures, dreams shattered, a break up with a boyfriend or girlfriend, made poor choices with money or time, found themselves stuck or facing a big choice. I have purposed to change for them so that I can remain a person they can depend on, if they need that. I try very hard not to tell them what to do, unless they ask. I listen a lot. I try to make myself available when they need me. I do not force the relationship. I do not tell them what to do any more. They are no longer in my home; they are making their own choices and living life.

My daughter is married and that brings a whole new level of letting them live their lives as I stay out of their marriage. I do not get involved in their finances, what they purchase, or their disagreements. I do not insist they come over; I purpose to go to them. I do not control holidays; I give them the choice. I learned how to parent this way from God, my Dad. He does this with us; He lets us walk through life and is always available when we need Him, and is a significant help if we ask. He does not force Himself on us, and so I try very hard not to force myself on my children. The more time I spend with God, the better I get at this. It is not easy, at times, but I keep my mouth shut as much as possible, unless asked.

The first two years that my son was in college in Florida, I hardly heard from him. I would get a call maybe once a month. I would send him a text (that is how he communicates) telling him that I love him and I was thinking about him. I always let him know that I am his biggest fan and believe in him, and that I am proud of him. Most of the time, I would hear nothing back, and I was okay with that. As I sat with the Lord about it, He showed me that he did not want to call because I was always trying to tell him what he should or should not do. I was questioning his choices. I was giving unsolicited advice and he did not want to hear it. I asked the Lord to help me change. As I stopped giving advice that was not asked for, the calls became more frequent. If I started to give advice, I would hear, "I gotta go, mom." I would forgive myself and try again. Eventually, I learned to change my attitude, thoughts, and words when we talked. I changed for him and did not insist he would change for me.

Another thing I found very helpful was I changed how I communicate. I learned how to text because they, my children, were texting. I did not force them to call me or communicate the way I preferred; I changed to what they preferred. I step into what they like to do, and let go of what I like to do. I change to understand and remain a part of their ever-changing world. If they communicate on Facebook, then I was on Facebook. By changing myself to be in their world, I am not being passed by with technology. I might not be up on every latest piece of technology, but I value what they know and do not criticize the change; I change with it on purpose. I am very intentional about changing with my children.

The best gift we can give our children is to change as they change. Release more and more responsibility to them to learn while they are in our home, and to learn we are the safety net, not the leash. I have had to do serious work on my heart to learn this. The more healed my heart and mind get with forgiving things of my past, the easier changing with my children becomes. We do not want our children to make the same mistakes we made at their age. We want to give them what we have learned from our mistakes, and yet, we miss the fact that we learned from our own mistakes, and they do to. The more I have worked on my past, the less I fear, which then helps me not to feel the need to control them. The healthier my relationship becomes with God, the healthier it becomes with my children. Let them live their lives and change with them and for them...

CHAPTER 12
Heart Change

There is nothing like being in a complete change of life with selling two houses, buying a house, a son graduating from college and getting engaged, to shake things up a bit in my heart...change reveals my heart. His word tells us to be anxious for nothing, but I seem to have a lot of anxiety. It is hard to get to sleep and hard to stay asleep. At the moment, I feel like I cannot add one more thing to my plate of life, and yet, things keep getting added to it. I do not personally like what I see coming out of me right here in the middle of it.

We have a tenant who did not pay his rent last month and it is now the 5th of the next month and he still has not paid. Oh yes, he has made promises and he said it was in the mail, and has given me excuse after excuse, and still no check. What has been surprising to me is how I have handled it. I have been very angry each time the check does not show up in the mailbox like he said.

Anger that should not be at this level for the offense I am experiencing. I did not want to hear his name and did not want to even think about him. I hate to admit that I did not even think to pray for him. I was plain angry. I kept trying to forgive him and I could get the anger to subside, but only until the next time I heard another excuse and no check.

So, I finally sought the Lord about my heart. I knew I was not handling all of this very well. I could have come up with many justifiable excuses as to why I was acting this way, but the truth is, I should not be acting this way. I am not saying that I was cussing and swearing at him, nor was I really outwardly angry with breaking or throwing things, but I was angry inside. The last excuse the tenant gave was that his child was in the hospital and he sent me a picture.

The Lord told me that I did not even pray for him. I was so focused on all of the lies and not paying that I did not even pray for his son in the hospital. Of course, the Lord heard my excuse that I did not believe him. I asked the Lord what in the world is wrong with my heart. I repented for not praying and for all of the anger.

Then, the Lord told me that I had "heart debt". What in the world is "heart debt"? He showed me I have kept an account in my heart of all of the people over the years who have not paid us. There were many people who I trusted and believed and they never paid. Wow, I did not even know it was in there. Every time this tenant was telling me something and I believed it, and then it did not happen, it was touching this debt in my heart. I was so focused on the present issue and the fact that he was not paying, I missed where it was going inside of me.

So, I sat there and allowed the Lord to open up the accounts of debt in my heart, person after person, and their debt owed to us. I forgave each of them from a depth I had not known. I handed the debt to Him as I forgave. I was surprised at how many people were in there, but I kept going until they were all gone. Then, I got a text that the checks had not arrived, yet again, but this time, no anger rose up inside of me. I was able to think clearly and address it properly. Wow, how did that happen? This current action was no longer able to join forces with past issues of my heart. My heart had changed.

Was He making all of this happen? I do not know, but I do know that I was in the middle of Him making all things work together for His good (Romans 8:28). I do know that my attitude was not right and my flesh was ruling. I do know that my focus was on him not paying, so much so that I was not even praying for him. I do know that I had a lot of debt from people stored up in my heart and this exposed it. I was even able to pray for them this morning. I was praying for their souls, and repenting that I was not a better example of His love toward them.

Do you have "heart debt"? Have you been dealing with a current issue and deep inside you know you should not be responding the way that you are, but you do not know why? It might be that you have debts or accounts in your heart from the past and this is poking at them. Ask the Lord if you need a heart change...I certainly did. Change and people, help us see what we cannot see about ourselves, if we have the courage to ask and look...

CHAPTER 13
Change Reveals

As I sit here writing this, we are getting ready to move to another home in a couple months, in another city, and on top of all of that, we are moving into a place less than half the size we are currently living in. At times, I am hard pressed on every side, fighting being overwhelmed with all there is to do with packing, changing addresses, neighbors, new friends, a new church, new stores, and everything else...

I have been paying attention to what this is doing inside of me. I noticed a few weeks ago that I was filled with fear. This fear was directed at my husband. I was getting all worked up inside. When we are afraid, we have a tendency to control. It was an unreasonable fear. When I sought the Lord about how I was thinking and treating my husband, He showed me un-forgiveness. Eleven years ago, we sold just about everything we had and moved across the United States. The day we loaded up what was left to take across, I felt my husband loaded all of his tools and treasures into the truck first, and when we got to the rest of the stuff, there was not room for some of it, so it got left behind. Because I did not forgive my husband for what I thought he did, I was holding it against him.

Was I aware of it over the last eleven years? No. But as we face moving into a smaller home, I was being triggered of the past. I was no way going to let him get all the space this time. I know this seems silly, but it was real; ask my husband. I was trying to tell him what he had to get rid of and what he could keep. He did surprisingly well with my attitude, but I was not okay with it. So, I went for a long walk and purposed to work on forgiving him for the perceived offense. He did not do it on purpose, but my mind remembered it that way.

I seriously forgave him repeatedly with the Lord, and I asked the Lord to forgive me and I forgave myself. I did not stop until I was free of what I was thinking. I went back to my husband and apologized for my irrational attitude. I told him he could keep whatever he felt he needed and I had no business getting involved in it (and I meant it). I was free! What changed? My heart let go of the offense of the past, and my perspective of the present was reasonable, when just moments before I was completely unreasonable.

Change gets us out of our habits. Our habits can keep us stuck and we do not even know it. Our habits can be established on lies and un-forgiveness, and until we are faced with change, it is not revealed because we can become very good at building walls around offenses of the past, and as long as everything stays the same, we can avoid the truth. We are usually not even aware of the fact that we are doing this...until we are faced with change...

Think about your life...how do you do if one part of your daily routine gets changed? Do you get frustrated? Do you get impatient? Do you find yourself easily irritated? What do you do about it? That change in the routine might be revealing something that needs your attention. Ask the Lord...

Maybe you are around someone who does not do well with change, like my husband was. Be gracious. If my husband had an unresolved issue of his own in this area, or with what I was telling him, we would have had a serious fight, thinking it was about what we were currently walking through, and yet, it was because of the past.

Do not avoid change, embrace it, allow it to reveal the hidden issues of your heart, and deal with them with the Lord...

CHAPTER 14
Get the FEAR Out

The other morning, I woke up surrounded by fear. It was real. It was consuming my mind. This was not the first time fear wanted to take over. It came as I was thinking about my day, and particularly thinking about the appraiser who was coming that day to appraise our home. We are in escrow to sell it, so an appraiser from the buyer's bank is necessary. I tried not to focus on it as I have in the past...still there. I played worship music and tried not to focus on it, as I have in the past...still there. I tried to ignore it, distract myself from it, and still it would not lift.

So, I decided to try something different...I faced it. I asked the Lord why I was afraid. What is it, Lord? I realized I was afraid that He was going to take it away, the sale, the move, the future, all of it... Wow, why was I thinking that? Then He showed me a moment over 11 years ago, when my husband and I had drove off to move our family to

South Carolina and our home had not sold. He told us to leave on June 18, and so we did, even when the house was still ours. It was a difficult time of faith. And then, in September, when we were out of our equity line to pay our bills, and it was the first day of ministry school, we got a call that we had an offer on our home. We were excited and asked the Lord about it. He told us these were the buyers and to accept the offer.

We did not totally obey what the Lord told us to do and we wrote a small counter offer back. They wanted us to pay $7,000.00 of their points for their loan. Their offer was for 1.2 million dollars for our home and we countered with paying only $3,500.00 of the points and the buyers just vanished. No one could get ahold of them. They were gone as fast as they came. WOW!

Two months later, we got another offer from them for a million dollars. We were not happy about it. In fact, we were offended that they would come back and offer $200,000 less than their original offer. We were mad and felt they were taking advantage of us. We knew we had to get over ourselves on this, but it was not easy. We were really mad at ourselves because we lost the original deal over $3,500.00 and here they were again.

We asked for 3 days to respond because we did not want to disobey the Lord again, and it was most likely going to take us at least 3 days to get over being upset. We ended up taking the exact offer and it was over...we thought...

This was the fear I was facing … was He going to take away these buyers. He did not take away the other buyers, but over the years, because I did not deal with the first issue and forgive the buyers, forgive my husband and myself, and repent and even forgive God, here it was again. These little situations of our past can continue to bring fear if we do not close the door by forgiving. I dealt with it and by the time the appraiser came, the fear and anxiety were gone.

Let's take this a step further…we know the Scriptures about fear in His word, 2 Timothy 1:7, "For God has not given us a spirit of fear, but of power and of love and of a sound mind." And 1 John 4:18, "There is no fear in love; but perfect love casts out fear, because fear involves torment. But he who fears has not been made perfect in love." We quote these Scriptures and try to convince ourselves not to fear, but the truth is, the fear only subsides and does not go away.

Un-forgiveness gives fear a place to stay. The enemy is always out to steal, kill, and destroy our relationship with God (John 10:10), who is love. When we choose not to forgive, we leave a door open for him to bring in doubt about God and who He is to us and for us. He, the enemy, knows if he can slowly erode our trust in God, one misperception at a time, we will have fear. If he, the enemy, can get us to think God is not with us or for us, or is out to get us, then we have fear. If he, the enemy, can twist the truth about a situation or how we remember it, then we have fear. Un-forgiveness in these little moments of decision making, or in events that happened to us, opens a door in the future for the enemy to bring fear like I wrote about above.

Sometimes fear gets in at a moment of trauma. A car accident, even when someone hides around a corner and jumps out, or something almost happens...you know what type of moments I'm talking about, where your heart beats so fast that you think it is going to burst...those moments are traumas where the enemy can bring in a spirit of fear. When those moments happen, forgive quickly to close the door. Forgive every one or thing involved, and do not forget to forgive yourself. This closes the door. If you have not done this with events in your life, take some time to close those doors by forgiving...Help your children, too...

Let me give you one more example...last year I was driving home and was at a traffic light. I took my foot off of the brake and was changing my regular glasses to sunglasses and all of a sudden I hit the car in front of me. I was pretty shaken up.

After all of the exchange of information and talking to the police, I drove home. I found myself filled with fear. I had not had a car accident for over 30 years, but all of a sudden, all of my confidence was gone in my ability to drive, and I was afraid. I asked the Lord why I was so afraid; I was hardly moving. He brought to mind two automobile accidents I had when I was 16 years old. One, I hit the car in front of me and pushed them into the car in front of them, and they were very upset with me. The second, a month later when I went off of a cliff while driving. I lost control because of some gravel and ended up going straight off of a cliff and tumbling down to the bottom of a ravine. I had not dealt with these two traumas, and so, there they were connecting with this minor accident and creating quite a bit of fear. I asked the Lord to forgive me for those accidents of my past and for agreeing with fear. I forgave myself and I literally felt the fear lift off of me. I was able to drive in that intersection with no fear. The door created from the traumas was closed and I was free.

Realize that fear is the absence of God's love. Fear is there because of un-forgiveness somewhere. Instead of ignoring the fear, or trying to avoid or push it away, face it; find out why it is there. Repent, forgive and forgive yourself and the fear dissipates. God does not bring this consuming fear, but situations do come where we are allowed to see it to deal with it. To get the FEAR out, face how it got there...and change...

CHAPTER 15
Fast to Change

If you are like me, you are not a huge fan of fasting. You might have stories of how hard it was in the past. Or maybe you have reasons why you cannot fast now. What do you think fasting is? Do you believe that fasting is just about not eating food? What if I told you that fasting was giving up something that has control over you other than God? What if fasting could change habits, mindsets, and behavior? What if fasting had the potential to change who you are right now? Are you interested?

Fasting is denying yourself of something that you feel has control over your time, your thoughts, your attitude, your choices, your responses, and your relationships, hence, affecting your relationship with God. This can be food, television, Facebook, our cell phone, being critical or negative, worry, books we are reading, drugs and alcohol, people we associate with that are not a good influence, and many other things that have control over us more than God. Things or habits that you want to change so that your relationship with Jesus can grow. Do you have any of those?

I have found that when the Lord asks me to give something up, it has more control over me than I realize. When I fast it, and it is hard, I discover its hold on me. Not that long ago, the Lord asked me to step away from Facebook. I thought it would be easy. I did not realize how that little notification sound had control of my actions. I realized I allowed it to interrupt conversations, my reading time in His Word, my prayer time, and my writing time. I had given it permission to interrupt me any time it wanted.

Wow, so simple, and yet, so controlling...He knew it had control I was not aware of. I was amazed at how much I accomplished in the day without Facebook. I had to allow those little numbers to grow on the screen of my phone and trust God with it. I had so much more time to focus on God. Wow, such a simple but effective change by fasting Facebook...

Have you ever wondered about this verse in Matthew 17:21, "However, this kind does not go out except by prayer and fasting." I think we view this as fasting food, but really Jesus has not taught that. So, what is He talking about fasting? What did He model? We know He modelled prayer because we hear about it all the time, but what is He talking about fasting? Did He fast? The disciples have tried to cast out a demon and could not and had come to Jesus to ask why...maybe there is more to this. Jesus did not let anything occupy His time that was not what the Father desired. Is Jesus talking about denying our flesh to rule? Is He talking about fasting (denying ourselves) what satisfies our flesh? Jesus did not allow His flesh to rule over anything, just look at His trial and journey to and on the cross. Think about it...

Do you know what rules over you? If you do not know, then ask the Lord to show you. Maybe you have a behavior you want to change, fast it (deny yourself having or doing it). Remember it is not easy if it has control over you instead of you having control over it. This is a great way to adjust things that need our self-control (Galatians 5:22-23, the last fruit of the Spirit) to actually control our self.

It might take some repentance and forgiving while in the process of fasting. I know I was asking the Lord to forgive me for giving Facebook so much more of my time than I should have. I repented for allowing it to interrupt my thoughts, and time with Him. I forgave myself, too. I will tell you that after fasting this, I felt so much more in control over my life, and my relationship with God had so much more depth. My time in His word was richer without all the interruptions.

As I am writing this, I think I need to do this again, because it has creeped back in. It is such a habit to just react to that little sound or number...back to fasting to change my choices...

Fast to change something that you do not like about yourself...

Fast to change what rules over you...

What do you need to fast to change? Be brave, tell it no, and enjoy the change!

CHAPTER 16
Testing Produces Change

"My brethren, count it all joy when you fall into various trials, knowing that the testing of your faith produces patience. But let patience have its perfect work, that you may be perfect and complete lacking nothing. If any of you lacks wisdom, let him ask of God, who gives to all liberally and without reproach, and it will be given to him" James 1:2-5. Testing produces change...whether we like it or not, it happens. Life produces many trials and tests and we have a choice as to what they actually do produce inside of us. We would like them to produce patience, but the process to be changed to a patient person is a difficult path, at least for me. Think about it, do you prefer to ask for wisdom or patience?

Over the last few months, my husband and I have been going round and round about the same thing and we have not been able to get on the same page, so to speak, about it. My husband has a great job and works very hard. He, at the moment, is working 12 hours a day, but does not record the overtime on his time sheet, so the boss is not aware of all of these hours. I kept encouraging him, my perception of my words, to write down what he is actually working. He continues not to do that, but did start recording a portion of it. Recently, they approached him to put him on salary. They based his salary according to the time he had recorded. I was frustrated and did not choose to keep my mouth shut about how I felt about it. I keep trying to forgive him so I am not so consumed with it, and this morning, I finally started getting a different perspective of it.

Instead of telling him how I felt about it, I needed to ask him how he felt about it. Instead of focusing on what I felt he was not doing, I needed to focus on what he was doing. Instead of complaining, I needed to build him up. I needed to appreciate his job. I needed to appreciate what he was getting paid and how hard a worker he is. I needed to focus on what a company man he is. All I was doing by complaining was adding to his pressure. I really do not know what he has to go through each day. Although, I feel he should focus on what he is getting paid, he is focusing on his job. As I have been forgiving, my thinking is changing. I had thought I was helping him, and instead, I was hindering him.

I was in the middle of a trial and testing of my faith, and I was fighting it with all that was within me, and I am finally beginning to see how to change what I am doing to help my husband. The more patient I get, the better a wife I can be. I had to forgive my husband, his work, and ask the Lord to forgive me, and yes, I had to forgive myself. The bottom line of the whole situation is that I was not trusting God with my husband's job and what he should or should not get paid.

This is a specific example, but where do you need to change? What does the Lord want to perfect in you? What have you been wrestling with for months or even years? He wants us to fully trust Him in every situation, and He knows where we are not. Un-forgiveness hinders us from this being produced in us. Where do you need to forgive? Are you given to change into what He sees as best for you?

I have been wrestling with this for months and seeking His word and asking Him to please help me. I have been embracing Romans 12:1-2, "I beseech you therefore, brethren, by the mercies of God, that you present your bodies a living sacrifice, holy, acceptable to God, which is your reasonable service. And do not be conformed to this world, but be transformed by the renewing of your mind, that you may prove what is that good and acceptable and perfect will of God." I have been wrestling with how the world thinks (conforming) about pay and work, and not allowing the situation to actually transform my thinking, increase my faith and trust in God, and be the wife God created and needs me to be for my husband. This is my reasonable service. This wrestling has been positioning me to be transformed; I just had to submit to it.

He is given to changing me (Philippians 1:6, "being confident of this very thing, that He who has begun a good work in you will complete it until the day of Jesus Christ".); I need to submit to being changed. He is not given to changing me as I was trying to change my husband, but He changes me as I submit to Him by forgiving, by resisting the devil by forgiving, and my trust in Him grows and my mind becomes renewed. I was creating my own trial and it would not have been necessary if I had trusted God with it. As I press into His word for help, it releases life into my thinking…I am given to change and His word changes me…

*My hope and prayer is that this book has deeply touched your heart. I pray as you embrace change with the Lord as I have, you, too, will experience deep freeing change in every area of your life...To God be the glory...
Great things He has done!!*

Do You Need Jesus?

If, for some reason, you have received this book and you do not know Jesus as your personal Savior, I want you to know that you can. I want you to know that there is nothing you have done that He will not forgive, if you ask Him.

Just say this simple prayer to begin your amazing journey with Jesus...

Dear Jesus,

Thank You for loving me and for dying on the cross for me. I ask that You please forgive me of my sins and that You come into my heart. I need You and want to get to know You.
I want the love You came to give.
Show me who You are.
I want to love You.

In Jesus' name. Amen.

It is that simple.

Welcome to the family of God!

May I encourage you to please get connected with a local church family that will help you learn more about what you have just done. If you do not know of one, please contact me and I will help you find one.

About the Author

Cheryl Stasinowsky is a speaker and writer of passion and transparency. Her desire is for others to see Jesus in everything they walk through; growing a new passion for His Word and its relevance for them. Please contact her to make arrangements for your future events, retreats, church services, meetings, and conferences.

She would love to meet you!

cheryl@wordscribeministries.com
www.wordscribeministries.com
www.hishiddentreasure.blogspot.com

Connect with Cheryl on Facebook and twitter @histreasures

What others are saying:

"Cheryl Stasinowsky is a treasure. Cheryl is a special artist that paints her teachings in faith constructionism, and as such, she passionately extracts the blueprints from the foundation of the Word and then builds that foundation into the details of everyday practical life. Her books and teachings are a life guide, and her speaking appearances are personal. She opens

herself to each person she is teaching, and lays out in honesty her own personal experiences of the presence of God within the joys and pains of everyday life."

"I have had the privilege of being ministered to and then later ministering with Cheryl for many years. She is a mighty woman of God who I love to call friend. She will give honest testimonials that are sure to share how God can triumph through all. Your congregation will receive kingdom keys for unlocking some of the mysteriousness oft felt when walking through hard things that are not Father caused, but are Father filtered. Ultimately, the listener will be left with an understanding that God is love and He will have victory in our lives if we let Him move through us."

"We were greatly blessed when Cheryl Stasinowsky came and spoke in our church, teaching us on operating in the gifts of the Spirit, particularly the prophetic. Not only did she bring anointed teaching but she also demonstrated and imparted the gifts of the Spirit to our congregation. This opportunity helped to bring our church into a new level of moving in the Spirit which has remained with us. I highly recommend Cheryl Stasinowsky as a speaker at your church or conference, not only is she gifted, she is also very humble and servant hearted which was such a refreshing deposit into all of our lives."

More Titles by Cheryl Stasinowsky

His Hidden Treasures

ISBN: 978-0-6158979-9-8

There is an unknown treasure sitting on your night stand, bookshelf or coffee table. It is full of keys that will unlock your destiny, vision and purpose. They are yours for the taking. Join Cheryl on this journey as she uncovers valuable secrets found in the Bible. Through her own brokenness and surrender, the author will inspire you to embark on your own journey of searching for the timeless and endless treasures in the Word of God. As you dig deeper, each hidden treasure will leave you desperate for more of God's Word.

Deeper Relevance

ISBN: 978-0-6159069-9-7

Cheryl set out to write a daily encouraging word on her social networks, not realizing that her pursuit for a deeper understanding of God's Word would blossom into a full devotional. Grab your Bible, along with this book, and get ready to discover kingdom nuggets that will enrich your walk and relationship with Jesus. His Word truly sustains us every day!

More Titles by Cheryl Stasinowsky

Now Faith

ISBN: 978-0-615899-07-7

Now Faith is a face-to-face encounter with the men and women of Hebrews 11 who had the kind of faith that pleased God and moved mountains. Each chapter steps inside their lives, takes a look around, finds vital parts of the DNA of their faith, and then supplies a prayer for the impartation of that faith.

Now Faith in Spanish (Es Pues, La Fe)

ISBN: 978-0-615899-67-1

Es Pues, La Fe es un encuentro, cara a cara, con los hombres y mujeres de Hebreos 11 quienes tuvieron la fe que agradó a Dios y que movió montañas. Cada capítulo toma un paso adentro de sus vidas, echa un vistazo a su forma de ser, encuentra partes vitales del ADN de su fe, y después suple una oración para la impartición de esa fe.

More Titles by Cheryl Stasinowsky

Private Moments With God

ISBN: 978-0-6159103-7-6

Life as we individually know it...Each of us has a past that is influencing how we see our present. We walk through our day with all of the pressures and demands of life with a past, in the present, and also with a hope for a future. I, too, journey this thing called life. Through it all, I have come to value to the highest degree the first moments of my early mornings when the house is quiet, it is still dark outside, my coffee is freshly brewed, my iPod is playing worship music in my ears, and I open the Word of God for my nourishment and encouragement for the day. These are those moments...

Given to Forgive

ISBN: 978-0-692306-60-4

Are you tired of wrestling with regret, guilt, anger, resentment, bitterness, and impatience? Did you know that all of these are symptoms of unforgiveness? I did not like to forgive and always thought that the other person had to come to me first to apologize. I held onto unforgiveness for years. Eight years ago, I started forgiving people, situations, and choices I had made. I hand you my journey of choosing to be given to forgive every day...

More Titles by Cheryl Stasinowsky

Given to Love

ISBN: 978-0-692485-51-4

It is not going to be what you think it is going to be. This is not a book on love as the world sees and shows love. This is a book on my journey through discovering how to love from His word working in and through me. I have purposed to try to put on His word and live love. I am still learning, but what I have learned, I give. It has been tested and tried and has hurt a lot. I have submitted to Him in difficult situations and have chosen to walk as He showed me and not how my flesh wanted to respond...I am Given to Love first over being right...Love wins!

Given to Prayer

ISBN: 978-0-692629-68-0

This book is written to bring greater understanding of prayer, and expose the lies that make it seem difficult. Prayer is conversation with God, that simple. We all seem to face times where prayer is a struggle and we feel He is not listening or answering. This book will change your view of prayer and your prayer life...

Coming soon ...

GIVEN TO LISTEN

All of Cheryl's books are available in
eBook and print versions on Amazon and Barnes & Noble.

www.ingramcontent.com/pod-product-compliance
Lightning Source LLC
Chambersburg PA
CBHW071520040426
42444CB00008B/1732